G A O
Accountability * Integrity * Reliability

Highlights

Highlights of GAO-11-802, a report to congressional committees

September 2011

CHESAPEAKE BAY

Restoration Effort Needs Common Federal and State Goals and Assessment Approach

Why GAO Did This Study

The Chesapeake Bay, with its watershed in parts of six states and the District of Columbia (watershed states), is an important economic and natural resource that has been in decline. Over decades, federal agencies and watershed states have entered into several agreements to restore the bay, but its health remains impaired. In May 2009, Executive Order 13508 established a Federal Leadership Committee, led by the Environmental Protection Agency (EPA), and directed the committee to issue a strategy by May 2010 to protect and restore the Chesapeake Bay (the Strategy). GAO was directed by the explanatory statement of the Consolidated Appropriations Act, 2008, to conduct performance assessments of progress made on bay restoration, and this first assessment examines (1) the extent to which the Strategy includes measurable goals for restoring the bay that are shared by stakeholders and actions to attain these goals; (2) the key factors, if any, federal and state officials identified that may reduce the likelihood of achieving Strategy goals and actions; and (3) agency plans for assessing progress made in implementing the Strategy and restoring bay health. GAO reviewed the Strategy, surveyed federal officials, and interviewed watershed state officials and subject matter experts.

What GAO Recommends

GAO recommends that EPA work with federal and state stakeholders to develop common goals and clarify plans for assessing progress. In commenting on a draft of this report, EPA generally agreed with the recommendations.

View GAO-11-802. For more information, contact David C. Trimble at (202) 512-3841 or trimbled@gao.gov.

What GAO Found

The *Strategy for Protecting and Restoring the Chesapeake Bay Watershed* includes 4 broad goals, 12 specific measurable goals with deadlines, and 116 actions to restore the bay by 2025. To achieve the broad and measurable goals, federal agencies, often in collaboration with the watershed states and other entities, are responsible for accomplishing the actions. However, not all stakeholders are working toward achieving the Strategy goals. The watershed states are critical partners in the effort to restore the bay, but state officials told GAO that they are not working toward the Strategy goals, in part because they view the Strategy as a federal document. Instead, most state bay restoration work is conducted according to state commitments made in a previous bay restoration agreement, the Chesapeake 2000 Agreement. Even though Strategy and Chesapeake 2000 Agreement goals are similar to some degree, they also differ in some ways. For example, both call for managing fish species, but the Strategy identifies brook trout as a key species for restoration and the Chesapeake 2000 Agreement does not. Federal and state officials said it is critical that all stakeholders work toward the same goals. The Federal Leadership Committee and the Chesapeake Bay Program—a restoration group established in 1983 that includes federal agencies and watershed states—created an action team in June 2010 to work toward aligning bay restoration goals. The two groups have accepted a process for developing common priorities and, if necessary, developing a new restoration agreement by 2013.

Officials from the 11 agencies responsible for the Strategy that GAO surveyed identified three key factors that may reduce the likelihood of achieving Strategy goals and actions: a potential lack of collaboration among stakeholders; funding constraints; and external phenomena, such as climate change. State officials and subject matter experts that GAO interviewed raised similar concerns. Federal officials reported that some form of collaboration is needed to accomplish the Strategy's measurable goals and the vast majority of its actions. In particular, federal-state collaboration is crucial, with federal officials indicating that collaboration with at least one state is necessary to accomplish 96 of the 116 actions in the 12 measurable goals. Federal officials also reported that funding constraints could reduce the likelihood of accomplishing 69 of the actions in 11 of the measurable goals. Furthermore, federal officials reported that external phenomena could reduce the likelihood that 8 of the measurable goals will be achieved.

The federal agencies have plans for assessing progress made in implementing the Strategy and restoring bay health, but these plans are limited or not fully developed, and it is unclear what indicators will be used to assess bay health. Per the Strategy, the agencies plan to create 2-year milestones for measuring progress made toward the measurable goals, with the first milestones covering 2012 and 2013. However, establishing milestones for an entire effort can improve the chances the effort can be accomplished efficiently and on time. Also, the Strategy states that the Federal Leadership Committee will develop a process for implementing adaptive management—in which agencies evaluate the impacts of restoration efforts and use the results to adjust future actions—but agency officials told GAO they are still developing this process. Moreover, there are now two groups that plan to assess bay health. The Strategy calls for the Federal Leadership Committee to coordinate with the watershed states to align these assessments. However, the status of this alignment is unclear, and if these groups use different indicators to assess bay health, confusion could result about the overall message of progress made.

_____ United States Government Accountability Office

Contents

Tables

Figures

Abbreviations

EPA   Environmental Protection Agency
TMDL   total maximum daily load

United States Government Accountability Office
Washington, DC 20548

September 15, 2011

The Honorable Jack Reed
Chairman
The Honorable Lisa Murkowski
Ranking Member
Subcommittee on Interior, Environment,
    and Related Agencies
Committee on Appropriations
United States Senate

The Honorable Mike Simpson
Chairman
The Honorable Jim Moran
Ranking Member
Subcommittee on Interior, Environment,
    and Related Agencies
Committee on Appropriations
House of Representatives

The Chesapeake Bay is the nation's largest estuary, and its watershed spans 64,000 square miles across six states—Delaware, Maryland, New York, Pennsylvania, Virginia, and West Virginia—and the District of Columbia, which we collectively refer to as watershed states. The bay provides habitat for a wide variety of animals and plants and supports local and regional economies. However, concerns about the bay's overall health surfaced as early as the 1930s, and signs of deterioration—declines in water clarity, dwindling oyster populations, and degraded habitat—became even more apparent in the 1950s and 1960s. In the 1970s and early 1980s, the Environmental Protection Agency (EPA) found that the primary causes for the decline in the bay's condition were excess nutrients from agriculture, such as nitrogen and phosphorus; population growth; and discharges from sewage treatment plants. More recently, a 2009 bay health assessment found that despite small improvements in certain areas, the bay continues to have poor water quality, low populations of many fish and shellfish species, and degraded habitats.[1]

Responding to public outcry about the degraded state of the bay, EPA and several watershed states first entered into an agreement in 1983 to restore and protect the bay. Through this agreement, these states and EPA began to work together as the Chesapeake Bay Program, a partnership that directs and conducts the restoration of the bay at the federal, state, and local levels, and also includes academic institutions and nonprofit organizations. Since then, EPA and several watershed states have entered into additional bay restoration agreements. The most recent agreement, Chesapeake 2000, set out an agenda and goals to guide restoration and protection efforts from 2000 through 2010 and beyond, and each of the watershed states made commitments to it. However, in October 2005, we reported that the success of the restoration effort had been undermined, in part by the lack of a comprehensive, coordinated implementation strategy and integrated approaches to measure overall progress.[2] We recommended that EPA should, among other things, work with the Bay Program to develop an overall, coordinated implementation strategy and develop and implement an integrated approach to assess overall restoration progress. Subsequently, the explanatory statement accompanying the Consolidated Appropriations Act, 2008, directed EPA, as the lead federal agency in the Bay Program, to immediately implement all of our recommendations and to develop a Chesapeake Bay action plan for the remaining years of the Chesapeake 2000 Agreement.[3] In response, the Bay Program submitted a report to Congress describing the steps it took to implement our recommendations. We testified in July 2008 that the Bay Program had taken positive steps, such as identifying key indicators for measuring bay health and restoration progress, to improve the coordination and

---

[1]Chesapeake Bay Program, *Bay Barometer: A Health and Restoration Assessment of the Chesapeake Bay and Watershed in 2009* (Annapolis, MD: April 2010).

[2]GAO, *Chesapeake Bay Program: Improved Strategies Are Needed to Better Assess, Report, and Manage Restoration Progress*, GAO-06-96 (Washington, D.C.: Oct. 28, 2005).

[3]House Appropriations Committee Print, Consolidated Appropriations Act, 2008, Pub. L. No. 110–161 Div. F at 1256; Consolidated Appropriations Act, 2008, Pub. L. No. 110-161, § 4 (2007).

management of the restoration effort, but that additional actions were needed.[4]

In May 2009, the administration stated that, despite decades of efforts by federal agencies, state and local governments, and other interested parties, bay restoration was not expected for many years. As a result, the President issued Executive Order 13508 to take further actions to restore and protect the bay.[5] The executive order established a Federal Leadership Committee to oversee the development and coordination of federal restoration programs and activities and called for the development by May 2010 of a strategy to protect and restore the bay. The Federal Leadership Committee is chaired by the EPA Administrator, and includes senior representatives from the U.S. Departments of Agriculture, Commerce, Defense, Homeland Security, the Interior, and Transportation. The executive order noted that although the federal government should assume a strong leadership role in the restoration of the bay, success depends on a collaborative effort involving each watershed state, local governments, and other organizations. The order stated that the committee shall consult extensively with the watershed states in the development of the strategy to ensure that federal actions are closely coordinated with actions by state and local agencies and that resources; authorities; and expertise of federal, state, and local agencies are used as efficiently as possible. The committee issued the *Strategy for Protecting and Restoring the Chesapeake Bay Watershed* (the Strategy) in May 2010.[6]

The explanatory statement accompanying the Consolidated Appropriations Act, 2008, directed EPA to develop a Chesapeake Bay action plan and GAO to conduct periodic performance assessments of progress made on this plan. Because EPA officials told us that the Strategy is the current plan to restore the bay, as agreed with your

---

[4]GAO, *Chesapeake Bay Program: Recent Actions Are Positive Steps Toward More Effectively Guiding the Restoration Effort,* GAO-08-1033T (Washington, D.C.: July 30, 2008).

[5]Executive Order 13508, Chesapeake Bay Protection and Restoration, 74 Fed. Reg. 23099 (May 15, 2009).

[6]Federal Leadership Committee for the Chesapeake Bay, *Executive Order 13508 Strategy for Protecting and Restoring the Chesapeake Bay Watershed* (Washington, D.C.: May 2010).

offices, this first performance assessment in response to the mandate focuses on the Strategy. This report examines (1) the extent to which the Strategy includes measurable goals for restoring the Chesapeake Bay that are shared by stakeholders and actions to attain these goals; (2) the key factors, if any, federal and state officials identified that may reduce the likelihood of achieving Strategy goals and actions; and (3) agency plans for assessing progress made in implementing the Strategy and restoring bay health.

To determine the extent to which the Strategy includes measurable goals for restoring the Chesapeake Bay that are shared by stakeholders and actions to attain these goals, we reviewed the Strategy to understand its structure and identify goals and actions. For the actions, we focused on the 116 actions that are designed to lead directly to the Strategy's goals. We also reviewed previous bay restoration agreements, such as Chesapeake 2000, to identify previous bay restoration goals. In addition, we interviewed federal and watershed state officials and representatives of organizations involved with bay restoration to gain an understanding of the Strategy and bay restoration efforts. To examine the key factors federal and state officials identified that may reduce the likelihood of achieving Strategy goals and actions, we conducted an electronic survey of the 11 federal agencies responsible for creating and implementing the Strategy: EPA; the Department of Agriculture's Forest Service and Natural Resources Conservation Service; the Department of Commerce's National Oceanic and Atmospheric Administration; the Department of Defense's Navy and U.S. Army Corps of Engineers; the Department of Homeland Security; the Department of the Interior's Fish and Wildlife Service, National Park Service, and U.S. Geological Survey; and the Department of Transportation. In addition, we interviewed officials from each watershed state to obtain their views on factors that could reduce the likelihood of achieving Strategy goals and actions. We also interviewed a nonprobability sample of members of academia with bay-related subject matter expertise. Because we used a nonprobability sample, the information obtained from these interviews is not generalizable to other members of academia with bay-related expertise. However, these interviews provided us with information on these individuals' views on the attainability of the Strategy's measurable goals. We selected these experts primarily through GAO's prior Chesapeake Bay work. To examine what plans are in place to assess progress made in implementing the Strategy and restoring the bay, we reviewed the Strategy and Strategy-related assessment documents and interviewed federal officials. A complete description of our scope and methodology is in appendix I. The questions from our electronic survey of federal agency officials are available in appendix II.

We conducted this performance audit from August 2010 to September 2011 in accordance with generally accepted government auditing standards. Those standards require that we plan and perform the audit to obtain sufficient, appropriate evidence to provide a reasonable basis for our findings and conclusions based on our audit objectives. We believe that the evidence obtained provides a reasonable basis for our findings and conclusions based on our audit objectives.

Background

The Chesapeake Bay is the nation's largest estuary, measuring nearly 200 miles long and 35 miles wide at its widest point. The bay's watershed covers 64,000 square miles and, as shown in figure 1, spans parts of six states—Delaware, Maryland, New York, Pennsylvania, Virginia, and West Virginia—and the District of Columbia. The Chesapeake Bay tributaries and watershed make up one of the most biologically productive systems in the world, with more than 3,600 species of plants, fish, and wildlife. The ecosystem also provides a variety of benefits to the almost 17 million people who live in the watershed, such as protecting drinking water, minimizing erosion and flood events related to stormwater runoff, and numerous recreational opportunities.

Figure 1: Chesapeake Bay Watershed

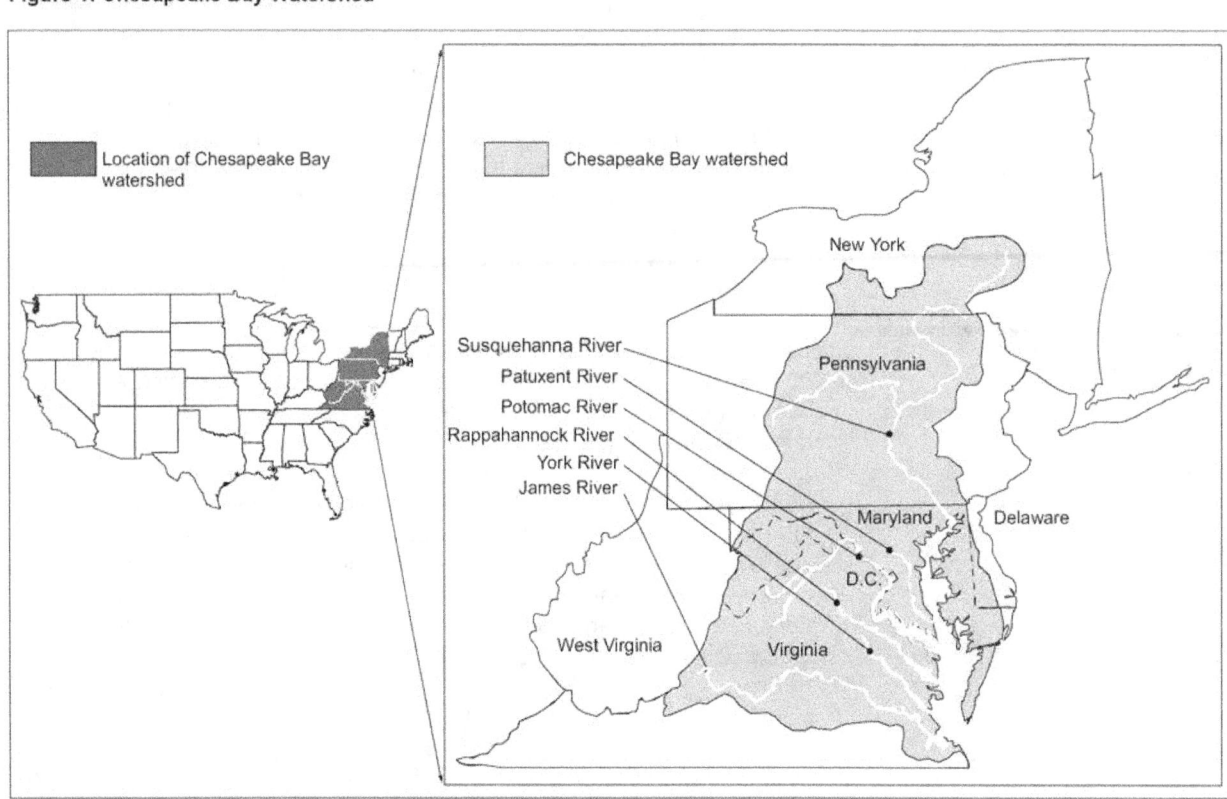

Sources: EPA and GAO.

Over time, however, the bay's ecosystem has deteriorated. As mentioned previously, water quality has deteriorated primarily because of excess amounts of nutrients entering the bay, which lead to the damage of animal and plant populations. According to a 2010 EPA bay document, the single largest source of these pollutants is agricultural runoff. In addition, population growth and development have further stressed the ecosystem.[7] The population of the bay watershed has doubled since 1950, adding approximately 1.5 million people every decade, and is

---

[7]EPA, *Chesapeake Bay Compliance and Enforcement Strategy* (Washington, D.C.: May 2010).

expected to approach 20 million by 2030. With this population increase, open spaces are being paved and developed, creating hardened surfaces that send an increasing amount of polluted stormwater into the bay and its rivers. Furthermore, sediment in the bay, stemming in part from agriculture and urban lands, has had harmful effects on the bay and its watershed, such as preventing light from penetrating to the leaves and stems of underwater grasses that provide habitat and stability to the bay.

The deterioration of the bay's ecosystem has been the cause for a great deal of public and political attention. Efforts to manage the bay's ecosystem and protect its living resources began as early as the 1930s and continue today. These efforts include the following:

- In 1980, Maryland and Virginia, later joined by Pennsylvania, established the Chesapeake Bay Commission to serve as an advisory body on the Chesapeake Bay to their state legislatures and as a liaison to Congress.

- In 1983, Maryland, Virginia, Pennsylvania, the District of Columbia, EPA, and the Chair of the Chesapeake Bay Commission signed the first Chesapeake Bay agreement, formalizing the Chesapeake Bay Program. The Bay Program is a partnership of federal agencies, states, academic institutions, and others that directs and conducts the restoration of the bay. EPA represents the federal government within the Bay Program and supports the partnership through its Chesapeake Bay Program Office. The signatories to the agreement reaffirmed their commitment to restore the bay in 1987 and again in 1992.

- In 2000, the Bay Program signatories signed the most current agreement, known as the Chesapeake 2000 Agreement. It outlined five broad goals and 102 commitments for the restoration effort. Delaware, New York, and West Virginia later signed a memorandum of understanding agreeing to work cooperatively to achieve the pollution reduction targets identified to meet the water quality goals in the agreement. The end dates in the Chesapeake 2000 Agreement commitments largely expired in 2010 or earlier. Some of these commitments have been renewed, but many have not.

- Also in 2000, Congress passed the Estuaries and Clean Waters Act, which directed EPA to take various actions to coordinate the Chesapeake Bay Program and to support the implementation of the Chesapeake 2000 Agreement. The act also required other federal agencies with facilities in the bay watershed to participate in restoration efforts.

In 2005, we examined the Bay Program's implementation of the Chesapeake 2000 Agreement to determine, among other things, the extent to which appropriate measures for assessing restoration progress had been established and how effectively the effort was being coordinated and managed.[8] Among other things, we found that the Bay Program lacked a comprehensive, coordinated implementation strategy to better enable it to achieve the goals outlined in the agreement and assessment reports did not effectively communicate the status of the bay's health. We made several recommendations to the Administrator of EPA, including to instruct the Chesapeake Bay Program Office to (1) work with the Bay Program to develop a comprehensive, coordinated implementation strategy and (2) to develop and implement an integrated approach to assess overall restoration progress. EPA took several actions to incorporate our recommendations, such as reducing more than 100 bay health and restoration indicators into three indices of ecosystem health and five indices of restoration effort.

Subsequently, in the explanatory statement of the Consolidated Appropriations Act, 2008, Congress directed EPA to implement immediately all the recommendations in our report, and to develop a Chesapeake Bay action plan for the remaining years of the Chesapeake 2000 Agreement. The Bay Program responded to the Consolidated Appropriations Act with a July 2008 report to Congress that described the program efforts to implement our recommendations, and the development of an action plan for the Chesapeake Bay.[9] We testified in July 2008 that the Bay Program had taken several actions in response to our recommendations, such as developing a strategic framework to unify planning documents and identify how it will pursue its goals.[10] However, we also testified that additional actions were needed before the program had the comprehensive, coordinated implementation strategy we recommended.

---

[8]GAO-06-96.

[9]EPA, Chesapeake Bay Program Office, *Strengthening the Management, Coordination, and Accountability of the Chesapeake Bay Program* (Annapolis, MD: July 2008).

[10]GAO-08-1033T.

On May 12, 2009, the President issued Executive Order 13508, Chesapeake Bay Protection and Restoration. The executive order noted that despite significant efforts, water pollution in the Chesapeake Bay prevents the attainment of state water quality standards, and that restoration of the bay was not expected for many years. It also stated that bay restoration will require restoring habitat and living resources, conserving lands, and improving management of natural resources. The executive order established the Federal Leadership Committee and required the committee to develop a strategy to guide efforts to restore and protect the bay. According to the order, the strategy was to define environmental goals for the Chesapeake Bay and describe the specific programs and strategies to be implemented, among other things. The Federal Leadership Committee published the Strategy in May 2010.

On December 29, 2010, EPA established a total maximum daily load (TMDL)—a "pollution diet"—for the Chesapeake Bay and the region's streams, creeks, and rivers in response to consent decrees stemming from litigation against the agency.[11] A TMDL is the calculation of the maximum amount of pollution a body of water can receive and still meet state water quality standards, and the Clean Water Act requires the creation of TMDLs for water bodies not attaining their water quality standards. The bay TMDL was also influenced by a settlement resolving a lawsuit filed against EPA in which the Chesapeake Bay Foundation and other entities alleged that EPA had failed to comply with the Clean Water Act by not taking steps to achieve some of the Chesapeake 2000 Agreement goals.[12] The bay TMDL is the largest ever developed by EPA, encompassing the entire 64,000-square-mile watershed. It identifies the necessary pollution reductions from major sources of nitrogen, phosphorus, and sediment across the District of Columbia and large sections of Delaware, Maryland, New York, Pennsylvania, Virginia, and West Virginia, and sets pollution limits necessary to meet water quality standards in the bay and its tidal rivers. To implement the TMDL, EPA is taking steps to ensure that each watershed state develops a Watershed Implementation Plan that details how and when it will meet pollution

---

[11]See *American Canoe Association v. United States Environmental Protection Agency*, 30 F.Supp.2d 908 (E.D.Va.1998); *Kingman Park Civic Association v. United States Environmental Protection Agency*, 84 F.Supp.2d 1 (D.D.C. 1999).

[12]The Chesapeake Bay Foundation is a nongovernmental organization that works with government, business, and citizens to protect and restore the bay.

allocations laid out in the TMDL. Each watershed state submitted its phase one implementation plan to EPA for review in November 2010, and must submit a phase two plan by March 2012 and a phase three plan in 2017.[13] If EPA concludes that a watershed state has taken insufficient steps to implement its Watershed Implementation Plans or to reduce pollution, the agency is prepared to take one or more actions, including expanding coverage of wastewater permits to sources that are currently unregulated.[14] The TMDL marks a change from the historic nature of the effort, which was based primarily on stakeholder agreements.

Restoration Strategy Includes Measurable Goals and Actions to Achieve Them, but Not All Bay Restoration Stakeholders Are Working toward These Goals

The Strategy articulates broad restoration goals, specific measurable goals, and actions to achieve those goals. Specifically, it includes 4 broad goals, 12 measurable goals with deadlines, and 116 actions to restore the bay by 2025.[15] The 4 broad goals—restore clean water, recover habitat, sustain fish and wildlife, and conserve land and increase public access—are identified in the Strategy as the most essential priorities for a healthy Chesapeake system. To meet these 4 broad goals, the Strategy identifies 12 measurable goals that contain numeric descriptions of results—or outcomes—to be achieved by 2025 (see table 1). For example, to help meet the recover habitat broad goal, the Strategy identifies a fish passage measurable goal to restore historical fish migratory routes by opening 1,000 additional stream miles by 2025, with restoration success indicated by the presence of river herring, American shad, or American eel. The Strategy also identifies four supporting strategies—expand citizen

---

[13]The Watershed Implementation Plans are part of EPA's bay TMDL accountability framework. The watershed states were expected to propose how they would distribute allocations of nitrogen, phosphorus, and sediment among various sectors and demonstrate reasonable assurance that those allocations will be achieved and maintained in the phase one Watershed Implementation Plans. In the phase two plans, the states are expected to identify key local, state, and federal partners who will be involved in meeting the TMDL; how the states will work with those partners; and how progress by those partners will be tracked, among other things. In the phase three plans, the watershed states are expected to make any midcourse adjustments to pollution reduction strategies and propose refinements if necessary.

[14]In a lawsuit filed on January 10, 2011, the American Farm Bureau Federation contended that, among other things, EPA had overstepped its authority in issuing a bay TMDL. The National Association of Home Builders filed suit against EPA in June 2011 with similar claims challenging the TMDL as unlawful. These cases have been consolidated.

[15]The 12 measurable goals are called outcomes in the Strategy. We refer to outcomes as measurable goals in this report.

stewardship, develop environmental markets, respond to climate change, and strengthen science—that were designed, in part, to provide cross-cutting support for attaining the Strategy's broad goals.[16]

Table 1: Strategy Broad Goals and Their Associated Measurable Goals

Strategy broad goals	Strategy measurable goals
Restore clean water Reduce nutrients, sediment, and other pollutants to meet bay water quality goals for dissolved oxygen, clarity, and chlorophyll-a and toxic contaminants.	*Water quality.* Meet water quality standards for dissolved oxygen, clarity/underwater grasses, and chlorophyll-a in the bay and tidal tributaries by implementing 100 percent of pollution reduction actions for nitrogen, phosphorus, and sediment no later than 2025, with 60 percent of segments attaining standards by 2025.
	Stream restoration. Improve the health of streams so that 70 percent of sampled streams throughout the Chesapeake watershed rate three, four, or five (corresponding to fair, good, or excellent) as measured by the Index of Biotic Integrity by 2025.
	Agricultural conservation. Work with agricultural producers to apply new conservation practices on 4 million acres of agricultural working lands in high-priority watersheds by 2025 to improve water quality in the Chesapeake Bay and its tributaries.
Recover habitat Restore a network of land and water habitats to support priority species and to afford other public benefits, including water quality, recreational uses, and scenic value across the watershed.	*Wetlands.* Restore 30,000 acres of tidal and nontidal wetlands and enhance the function of an additional 150,000 acres of degraded wetlands by 2025.
	Forest buffer. Restore riparian forest buffers to 63 percent, or 181,440 miles, of the total riparian miles (stream bank and shoreline miles) in the bay watershed by 2025.
	Fish passage. Restore historical fish migratory routes by opening 1,000 additional stream miles by 2025, with restoration success indicated by the presence of river herring, American shad, or American eel.
Sustain fish and wildlife Sustain healthy populations of fish and wildlife, which contribute to a resilient ecosystem and vibrant economy.	*Oyster.* Restore native oyster habitat and populations in 20 tributaries out of 35 to 40 candidate tributaries by 2025.
	Blue crab. Maintain sustainable blue crab interim population target of 200 million adults (1+ years old) in 2011 and develop a new population rebuilding target for 2012-2025.
	Brook trout. Restore naturally reproducing brook trout populations in headwater streams by improving 58 subwatersheds from "reduced" classification (10-50 percent of habitat lost) to "healthy" (less than 10 percent of habitat lost) by 2025.
	Black duck. Restore a 3-year average wintering black duck population in the bay watershed of 100,000 birds by 2025.

---

[16]We did not evaluate these four supporting strategies, or the 51 actions associated with them, because the four supporting strategies do not have specific, measurable goals of their own, but rather are closely tied to achievement of the broad goals.

Strategy broad goals	Strategy measurable goals
Conserve land and increase public access	*Land conservation.* Protect an additional 2 million acres of land throughout the watershed currently identified as high conservation priorities at the federal, state, or local level by 2025, including 695,000 acres of forest land of highest value for maintaining water quality.
Conserve landscapes treasured by citizens to maintain water quality and habitat; sustain working forests, farms, and maritime communities; and conserve lands of cultural, indigenous, and community value. Expand public access to the bay and its tributaries through existing and new local, state, and federal parks; refuges; reserves; trails; and partner sites.	*Public access.* Increase public access to the bay and its tributaries by adding 300 new public access sites by 2025.

Source: GAO analysis of the Strategy.

In turn, the 12 measurable goals were designed to be achieved through the accomplishment of 116 actions. These actions describe activities to be taken by federal agencies, often in collaboration with the watershed states and other entities. For example, one action in the fish passage measurable goal—remove stream barriers and provide fish passage—calls for two federal agencies to work with state and local partners to, among other things, prioritize stream barriers that inhibit fish passage. Figure 2 illustrates the relationship of the recover habitat broad goal and its measurable goals and selected actions. Federal officials we surveyed reported that about 95 percent of the actions in the Strategy could definitely or probably be accomplished, assuming current and expected budget and staff levels, and generally agreed that accomplishing the actions will lead to the achievement of the measurable and broad goals by 2025.

Figure 2: The Recover Habitat Broad Goal and Its Measurable Goals and Actions

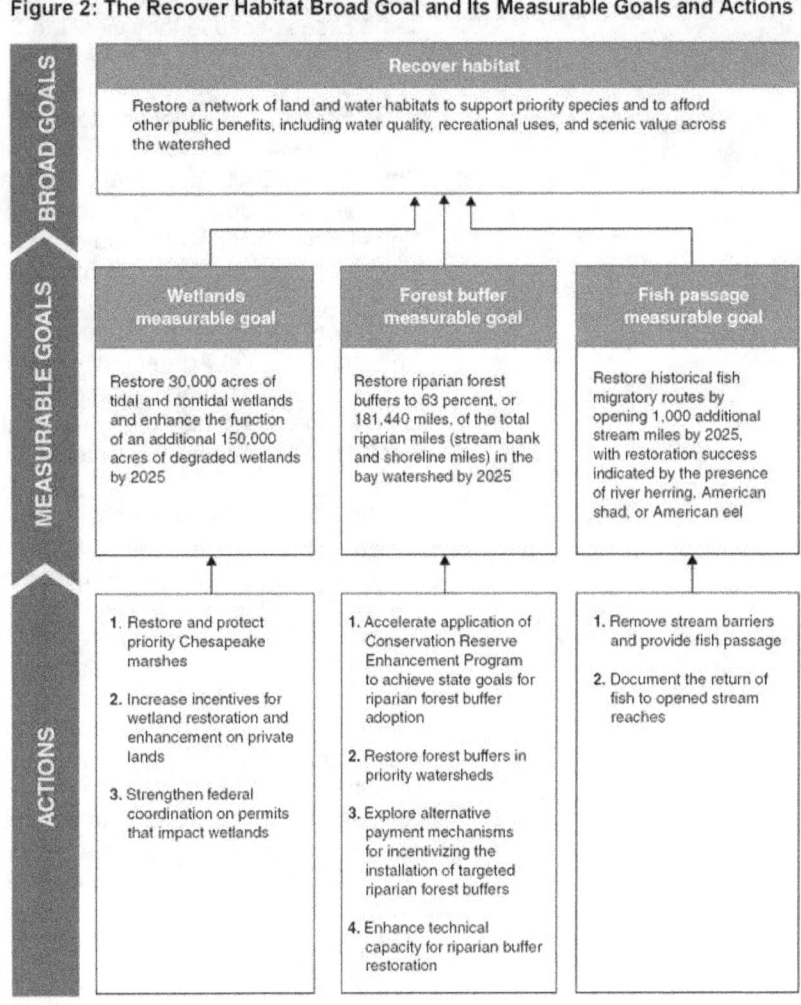

Source: GAO analysis of the Strategy.

Note: The recover habitat broad goal contains a total of 24 actions. In addition to the 9 actions listed, an additional 15 actions are identified in the Strategy to generally support the recover habitat broad goal and measurable goals.

Even though the federal agencies have developed a plan with measurable goals and actions, we found that not all stakeholders are working toward achieving these measurable goals. The watershed states are critical partners in the effort to restore the bay, but officials from each of the states told us that even though their states are conducting bay restoration work, their states are not working toward the Strategy goals, in some cases because they view the Strategy as a federal document. As of July 2011, the watershed states have not committed to the Strategy. Instead, most watershed state officials told us that their bay restoration work is conducted according to their commitments to the Chesapeake 2000 Agreement. Federal and state officials told us that Strategy and Chesapeake 2000 Agreement goals are similar to some degree. For example, both identify phosphorus and nitrogen reduction as necessary steps for improving water quality. However, the goals also differ in some ways. For example, both the Strategy and the Chesapeake 2000 Agreement call for managing fish species, but the Strategy identifies brook trout as a key species for targeted restoration efforts and the Chesapeake 2000 Agreement does not. Both agreements also have oyster restoration goals, but the Strategy identifies a number of tributaries to be restored and the Chesapeake 2000 Agreement focuses on an increase in the number of oysters in the bay.

In addition, officials from most of the watershed states told us that they are focused on accomplishing tasks associated with the bay TMDL, such as developing their Watershed Implementation Plans. Officials from several federal agencies also observed that the watershed states are fully occupied with efforts to comply with the TMDL. The bay TMDL was incorporated into the Strategy's water quality broad goal, which means that the pollution reduction steps that the states plan to implement in order to achieve the TMDL should contribute to the accomplishment of that Strategy goal. Similarly, each watershed state has identified pollution reduction activities in its phase one Watershed Implementation Plan that could contribute incidentally to other Strategy goals, even though the activities were created to achieve water quality standards and development on them began before the publication of the Strategy. For example, each watershed state has identified wetland restoration as part of its phase one Watershed Implementation Plan, and the Strategy's recover habitat goal contains a measurable goal to restore wetlands. However, it is unclear whether the watershed states' wetland restoration activities will be sufficient to help meet the Strategy's measurable goal for wetlands. For example, not all of the Watershed Implementation Plans identify the total wetland acreage to be restored.

It is important for all partners in the restoration effort to be working toward the same goals. We have previously reported that identifying common goals is a key characteristic of successful collaborative efforts.[17] Specifically, we found that having common goals, among other factors, can help lead to increased participation and cooperation among groups involved in a collaborative effort and to improve natural resource conditions. Several of the federal and state officials we interviewed also said that they believe it is critical that all stakeholders in the bay restoration effort are working toward the same goals and following the same plan. For example, a federal official told us that alignment between the Strategy and state actions would allow for the most integrated, efficient way of restoring the bay. In addition, a state official told us that the lack of alignment leads to a lack of support for the Strategy from the states.

In June 2010, the Federal Leadership Committee and the Bay Program created an alignment action team to work toward aligning Strategy restoration efforts with those of the Bay Program, including Chesapeake 2000 Agreement efforts. In addition to the lack of common goals, the team also identified several other reasons for alignment, including restoration tracking and communication difficulties caused by stakeholders focusing on different goals, and that limited resources are being diverted to addressing organizational confusion rather than implementation of bay restoration efforts. In January 2011, the alignment action team proposed developing a new restoration plan to provide a blueprint for the future of the restoration effort that will align Strategy and Bay Program goals. The Federal Leadership Committee and Bay Program have not yet agreed to develop this new plan. Under a process that was agreed to by both groups, they will work within preexisting Bay Program groups, called Goal Implementation Teams, to, among other things, refine priorities and areas of programmatic focus, guided by the Chesapeake 2000 Agreement and the Strategy. As part of this process, if the groups decide to negotiate a new agreement, it would not be negotiated until 2013, according to a July 2011 Bay Program document.

---

[17]GAO, *Natural Resource Management: Opportunities Exist to Enhance Federal Participation in Collaborative Efforts to Reduce Conflicts and Improve Natural Resource Conditions*, GAO-08-262 (Washington, D.C.: Feb. 12, 2008).

Federal and State Officials Identified Three Key Factors That May Reduce the Likelihood of Achieving Strategy Goals and Actions

Officials we surveyed from the 11 federal agencies responsible for the Strategy identified three key factors that may reduce the likelihood of achieving Strategy goals and actions, and state officials and subject matter experts we interviewed raised similar concerns. We identified as key those factors most frequently identified by federal officials: collaboration, funding constraints, and external phenomena.

Collaboration. First, most of the federal officials we surveyed indicated that a potential lack of collaboration among stakeholders could reduce the likelihood of achieving Strategy goals and actions. They reported that some form of collaboration is necessary to accomplish all of the Strategy's measurable goals and the vast majority of its actions. This collaboration could be between federal agencies, federal and state agencies, or federal agencies and other entities. In particular, federal-state collaboration is crucial to accomplishing the Strategy's goals and actions. In their survey responses, federal officials indicated that collaboration with at least one state is necessary to accomplish 96 of the 116 actions in all 12 of the measurable goals. For example, the Strategy's measurable goal for blue crab calls in part for the development of a new blue crab population target for 2012 through 2025, but a federal official reported that setting such a target is a matter of state, not federal, jurisdiction. The official indicated that the federal agency responsible for the action will facilitate state agreement on a new target, but that securing agreement is in the hands of the states, not the agencies. Table 2 shows the number of actions that, according to federal officials' survey responses, need state participation in order to be accomplished. Appendix III provides additional information on the extent to which collaboration between federal agencies and watershed states is needed to accomplish strategy actions.

Table 2: Number of the 116 Strategy Actions for Which Watershed State Participation Is Necessary to Accomplish Them, as Reported by Federal Officials

State	Number of actions
Maryland	94
Virginia	90
Pennsylvania	70
New York	65
Delaware	64
West Virginia	64
District of Columbia	52

Source: GAO analysis of survey responses.

Note: If more than one agency identified the same state as necessary for the same action, that action was counted only once for that state. The maximum number of actions for which each state's participation could be necessary is 116.

Even though the watershed states are critical partners in the restoration effort, most watershed state officials told us that they are generally unaware of what federal agencies may require of them to implement the Strategy. Specifically, officials from six of the seven watershed states noted that they were not aware of the extent to which federal agencies needed their participation when we told them the number of actions federal officials had identified that would need state participation to be accomplished. Some federal and state officials noted that their agencies are working on bay issues through the Goal Implementation Teams. Some of these groups are discussing the Strategy, but, according to a January 2011 Bay Program memorandum, specific state contributions toward the measurable goals have not been determined.

In addition to the need for federal-state collaboration, collaboration between two or more federal agencies is necessary to accomplish 40 of the actions in 8 of the measurable goals, according to our survey results. Some federal officials told us that collaboration among federal agencies increased during the development and implementation of the Strategy. According to some federal officials, this has resulted in closer relationships between some agencies and more tools and perspectives being used to restore the watershed. Other officials expressed concern that recent bay restoration meetings have focused largely on bay water quality issues with less time spent on other restoration activities and needs, such as restoring brook trout populations or increasing public access to the bay.

Funding constraints. The second key factor stakeholders identified that may reduce the likelihood of achieving Strategy goals and actions is funding constraints. Specifically, in their survey responses, federal officials indicated that funding constraints at the federal and state levels, and among other partners, such as academic institutions, could reduce the likelihood of accomplishing 69 of the actions in 11 of the measurable goals. Some federal officials told us that increased federal funding will be critical to accomplishing the actions and measurable goals. For example, a federal official reported that achieving the measurable goal for land conservation is contingent upon increased federal funding, in part because the recent economic crisis has reduced state land conservation funding. State land conservation funding is necessary to accomplish several land conservation actions in the Strategy, according to federal survey responses. In addition, another federal official told us that the measurable goal of restoring oyster habitat and populations has been delayed because of late allocations of fiscal year 2011 funding.

Officials from each of the watershed states also told us that funding constraints may reduce their ability to restore the bay. For example, officials from one state told us that their state needs about $38 billion in wastewater treatment infrastructure to reduce water pollution, and noted that overall challenging fiscal circumstances mean the state has a limited capacity to conduct additional bay restoration activities. Similarly, officials from another state told us that their state has experienced budget cuts in recent years and that funding constraints could reduce the likelihood of conducting restoration activities. In addition, fish passage experts we interviewed told us that states will have to contribute significant funding for stream restoration projects if the measurable goal of increasing fish passages is to be achieved. However, states' current fiscal conditions may reduce their ability to do so.

External phenomena. The third key factor that may reduce the likelihood of achieving Strategy goals and actions, according to federal agency survey responses and subject matter experts, is external phenomena that are outside the control of the agency, such as climate change or population growth. Even though the Strategy addresses some external phenomena, for example, by including a supporting strategy for responding to climate change, federal officials told us that effects beyond what was planned for in developing the Strategy could affect the likelihood of achieving the measurable goals. Specifically, federal officials reported that external phenomena could reduce the likelihood that 8 of the measurable goals will be achieved even if all of the actions in those measurable goals were accomplished. For example, according to one federal agency's survey response and a subject matter expert we interviewed, both climate change and increased development in the watershed could reduce the likelihood of achieving the measurable goal to restore naturally reproducing brook trout populations in headwater streams by 2025. The brook trout expert explained that climate change may affect stream temperature, which can result in a loss of brook trout. In addition, the expert told us that an increase in the amount of impervious surfaces in the watershed as a result of development can increase polluted runoff and degrade habitat, resulting in a loss of brook trout. As another example, insufficient or degraded breeding habitat outside of the bay watershed could reduce the likelihood of achieving the measurable goal of restoring a 3-year average wintering black duck population of 100,000 birds by 2025, according to this agency's survey response and two subject matter experts.

Agency Plans for Assessing Progress on Implementing the Strategy and Restoring Bay Health Are Limited or Not Fully Developed, and It Is Unclear What Indicators Will Be Used to Assess Progress on Bay Health

The Strategy calls for the federal agencies to, among other things, develop 2-year milestones, an adaptive management process, and annual progress reports to assess progress made in implementing the Strategy and restoring the health of the bay. However, the milestone development plan is limited, plans for adaptive management and the annual progress report are not fully developed, and it is unclear what indicators will be used to assess progress on bay health.

Milestone Development Plan Is Limited

The federal agencies do not plan to develop milestones for the entire Strategy period. Per the Strategy, the agencies plan to create milestones every 2 years for measuring progress made toward the measurable goals, with the first set of 2-year milestones to cover calendar years 2012 and 2013. However, setting the milestones every 2 years allows for the possibility of moving the target date to the next 2-year milestone period if the milestone could not be met in those 2 years, thereby prolonging the time it will take to meet the Strategy's goals. In addition, without a blueprint of milestones for the entire restoration effort, it is unclear how the agencies will determine whether they are on track to achieve the 12 measurable goals and 4 broad goals by 2025. Some restoration activities may not result in immediate improvements to the health of the bay, and it may be reasonable to expect slower progress toward a measurable goal initially, with faster progress made after a number of years into the restoration effort. On the other hand, some restoration activities may be easier to accomplish than others, and it may be reasonable to expect faster progress made toward a measurable goal initially and slower progress made after a number of years into the effort. By identifying a blueprint of milestones for the entire restoration effort, the agencies can show when the actions are expected to result in progress toward the measurable goals, determine whether these actions are having their intended result, and make changes to these actions if needed. We have reported that establishing milestones for an entire effort can improve the chances the effort can be accomplished efficiently and on time and provide decision makers with an indication of the incremental progress the agency expects to make in achieving results.[18]

Plans for Adaptive Management and Annual Progress Report Are Not Fully Developed

The Federal Leadership Committee has neither developed an adaptive management process nor identified what performance data it will use to gauge progress in the annual progress report. The Strategy states that the Federal Leadership Committee will develop a process for implementing adaptive management, but officials from EPA and other committee agencies told us that they are still developing this process. According to EPA officials, the Federal Leadership Committee agreed to the seven-step adaptive management decision framework that the Bay Program adopted in May 2011. This framework, however, was developed for the Bay Program and does not include clear linkages to the Strategy actions and measurable goals. It is unclear how it will be used by the Federal Leadership Committee agencies to adaptively manage Strategy actions and meet Strategy goals (see app. IV). In August 2011, EPA officials noted that a fully developed adaptive management process is needed. A fully developed adaptive management process should allow the agencies to evaluate whether Strategy actions are leading to the measurable goals and, if needed, adjust their efforts. This approach

---

[18]GAO, *South Florida Ecosystem Restoration: Substantial Progress Made in Developing a Strategic Plan, but Actions Still Needed*, GAO-01-361 (Washington, D.C.: Mar. 27, 2001), and *Agency Performance Plans: Examples of Practices That Can Improve Usefulness to Decisionmakers*, GAO/GGD/AIMD-99-69 (Washington, D.C.: Feb. 26, 1999).

includes assessing the problem, designing a plan that includes measurable management objectives, monitoring the impacts of the selected management actions, and evaluating and using the results to adjust management actions. In 2004, the National Research Council defined adaptive management as a process that promotes flexible decision making in the face of uncertainties, as outcomes from management actions and other events become better understood. In 2011, the National Research Council looked at the Chesapeake Bay Program's nutrient reduction program and found that neither EPA nor the watershed states exhibit a clear understanding of how adaptive management might be applied in pursuit of the Bay Program's water quality goals.[19] We believe a fully developed adaptive management process is essential to Strategy success because the agencies can improve bay restoration efforts by learning from management outcomes. We have previously reported that the lack of a well-developed adaptive management process impaired the success of collaborative restoration efforts, such as restoring the South Florida ecosystem and restricting bison movement in Montana to prevent the spread of disease.[20]

The Strategy also calls for the Federal Leadership Committee to develop an annual progress report that would, in part, assess the progress made in implementing the Strategy in the previous year. According to EPA officials, the agencies will report progress on the actions quarterly to the committee, and the agencies will use these quarterly reports to develop an annual progress report that will be issued to the public. In a fiscal year 2011 action plan, the Federal Leadership Committee identified which federal agency is responsible for implementing each Strategy action and what the agencies are expected to accomplish in that year.[21] The committee has also separately designated a lead federal agency for assessing progress toward each measurable goal, and that progress will

---

[19]National Research Council, *Achieving Nutrient and Sediment Reduction Goals in the Chesapeake Bay: An Evaluation of Program Strategies and Implementation* (Washington, D.C.: April 2011).

[20]GAO, *South Florida Ecosystem Restoration: Task Force Needs to Improve Science Coordination to Increase the Likelihood of Success*, GAO-03-345 (Washington, D.C.: Mar. 18, 2003), and *Yellowstone Bison: Interagency Plans and Agencies' Management Need Improvement to Better Address Bison-Cattle Brucellosis Controversy*, GAO-08-291 (Washington, D.C.: Mar. 7, 2008).

[21]Federal Leadership Committee for the Chesapeake Bay, *Fiscal Year 2011 Action Plan* (Washington, D.C.: Sept. 30, 2010).

also be included in the annual progress report. According to the Strategy, the Federal Leadership Committee plans to issue the first annual progress report in early 2012. The committee has not developed a template for the annual progress report, however, and federal officials were unable to tell us what performance data will be collected and reported in it to gauge progress. Performance information provided by the agencies in the first quarterly report on progress made during the first quarter of fiscal year 2011 varies. In some cases the report has no description of progress made on some actions, general information about steps taken toward some actions, and detailed information about progress made in others.

It Is Unclear What Indicators Will Be Used to Assess Bay Health

There are now two groups—the Federal Leadership Committee and the Bay Program—that plan to assess bay health. According to the Strategy, the committee's annual progress report will review indicators of environmental conditions in the bay, in addition to progress made in implementing the Strategy. In addition, since 2004, the Bay Program has assessed bay restoration progress through annual assessments of the health and restoration of the bay and its watershed, called the Bay Barometer.[22] Both the Federal Leadership Committee and the Bay Program plan to assess bay health in 2011 and publish these assessments in 2012. However, federal officials told us that they have not yet determined the content of next year's Bay Barometer report. It is therefore unclear if the Federal Leadership Committee and Bay Program will assess the same or different indicators of progress toward bay health.

Even though two different assessments of bay health in 2012 could present a consistent message of bay health, they could also result in confusion. For example, assessments based on different indicators could draw different, and possibly contradictory, conclusions about progress made in improving the overall health of the bay. The team created in June 2010 to align Strategy and Bay Program goals reported in January 2011 that the restoration effort is facing difficulty tracking progress and communicating that progress. The Strategy calls for the Federal Leadership Committee to coordinate with the watershed states to align

---

[22]EPA is responsible for issuing a report on the state of the bay ecosystem every 5 years, starting in April 2003, as directed by the Clean Water Act.

the annual progress report with the Bay Barometer, but, according to EPA officials, the status of this alignment is unclear.

Conclusions

Efforts to restore the Chesapeake Bay have been ongoing for several decades. The restoration effort has seen some successes in certain areas, but the overall health of the bay remains degraded. Restoring the bay is a massive, complex, and difficult undertaking that requires the concerted effort of many parties. Numerous federal and state agencies and others all play a role in the effort. To restore the bay in the most efficient and effective manner, these parties must work together toward the same goals. The Strategy that federal agencies developed for protecting and restoring the bay in response to Executive Order 13508 identifies measurable bay restoration goals and actions to achieve these goals. State participation in the Strategy is necessary to achieve these goals, yet the watershed states are not committed to the Strategy. Currently, federal agencies are generally working toward the Strategy goals, while states are largely focused on accomplishing tasks associated with the bay TMDL, which supports one of the Strategy goals. Having common goals, among other factors, can help lead to increased participation and cooperation among groups involved in a collaborative effort and improve natural resource conditions.

The Federal Leadership Committee and the Chesapeake Bay Program have recognized the need to align federal and state efforts to restore the bay. But regardless of how efforts are aligned, if the agencies do not identify milestones for accomplishing the entire restoration effort, they may not be able to show when particular actions are expected to result in progress toward measurable goals. Furthermore, the agencies have not yet developed an adaptive management process, which is essential to evaluating whether actions are leading to goals and make adjustments as necessary. In addition, the Strategy calls for the Federal Leadership Committee to coordinate with the watershed states to align Strategy and Bay Program assessments. However, the status of this alignment is unclear, and both the committee and Bay Program plan to assess bay health. If they use different indicators to assess and report, confusion could result about the overall message of progress made in improving the health of the bay, because assessments based on different indicators could draw different, and possibly contradictory, conclusions about the overall health of the bay.

Recommendations for Executive Action

To improve the likelihood that bay restoration is attained, we recommend that the Administrator of EPA work collaboratively with federal and state bay restoration stakeholders to take the following four actions:

- develop common bay restoration goals to help ensure that federal and state restoration stakeholders are working toward the same goals,

- establish milestones for gauging progress toward measurable goals for the entire restoration effort,

- develop an adaptive management process that will allow restoration stakeholders to evaluate progress made in restoring the bay and adjust actions as needed, and

- identify the indicators that will be used for assessing progress made in improving bay health and clarify how the entities responsible for assessing this progress will coordinate their efforts.

Agency Comments, Third-Party Views, and our Evaluation

We provided EPA and the Departments of Agriculture, Commerce, Defense, Homeland Security, the Interior, and Transportation with a draft of this report for their review and comment. We also provided the District of Columbia, Delaware, Maryland, New York, Pennsylvania, Virginia, West Virginia, and the Chesapeake Bay Commission with a draft of this report for their review and comment. EPA provided written comments and generally agreed with our recommendations. EPA also provided technical comments, which we incorporated as appropriate. Its written comments are reproduced in appendix V. The Department of Homeland Security provided written comments but did not comment on our recommendations. Its written comments are reproduced in appendix VI. The Department of the Interior disagreed with some of our findings and recommendations. Its written comments are reproduced in appendix VII. New York provided written comments but did not comment on our recommendations. New York also provided technical comments, which we incorporated as appropriate. Its written comments are reproduced in appendix VIII. The Departments of Agriculture and Transportation, the District of Columbia, and Virginia provided technical comments, which we incorporated as appropriate. The Departments of Commerce and Defense, Delaware, Maryland, Pennsylvania, West Virginia, and the Chesapeake Bay Commission had no comments.

EPA generally agreed with our four recommendations. In commenting on our recommendation that the Administrator of EPA work collaboratively with federal and state bay restoration stakeholders to develop common bay restoration goals, EPA noted that there is a new complexity regarding restoration goals given the development of the Strategy and that the completion dates for most Chesapeake 2000 Agreement commitments are set for 2010 or before. We agree. As we noted in the draft report, restoring the bay is a massive, complex, and difficult undertaking that requires the concerted effort of many parties. To restore the bay in the most efficient and effective manner, these parties must work together toward the same goals. Having common goals, among other factors, can help lead to increased participation and cooperation among the groups involved in the effort. In its comments, EPA stated that the draft report did not highlight where common goals and common directions are already present in the Chesapeake Bay Program. We noted in the draft report that the bay TMDL was incorporated into the Strategy's water quality broad goal, which means that the pollution reduction steps that the states plan to implement to achieve the TMDL should contribute to the accomplishment of the Strategy goal. In commenting on our recommendation that the Administrator of EPA work collaboratively with federal and state bay restoration stakeholders to establish milestones for gauging progress toward measurable goals for the entire restoration effort, EPA recognized that a blueprint of milestones through 2025 would be useful. EPA expressed concern about locking in a too detailed plan for the entire time period, because it does not wish to limit its ability for adaptive management. We believe that a blueprint of milestones can assist in the adaptive management process. As we noted in the draft report, a blueprint of milestones would allow agencies to show when the actions are expected to result in progress toward the measurable goals, determine whether these actions are having their intended result, and make changes to these actions as needed. We also reported that establishing milestones for an entire effort can improve the chances the effort can be accomplished efficiently and on time and provide decision makers with an indication of the incremental progress the agency expects to make in achieving results. In commenting on our recommendation that the Administrator of EPA work collaboratively to develop an adaptive management process that will allow restoration stakeholders to evaluate progress made in restoring the bay and adjust actions as needed, EPA acknowledged that this concern has been raised in previous GAO reports and in a recent National Academy of Sciences report. EPA also noted that a seven-step adaptive management decision framework was adopted by the Bay Program in May 2011 and endorsed by the Bay Program's leadership in July 2011. However, as we note in the report, this framework was developed for the Bay Program and does not include clear linkages to the Strategy actions and measurable goals. It is unclear how this framework will be used by the Federal Leadership Committee agencies to adaptively manage Strategy actions and meet Strategy goals. It is presented in appendix IV. In commenting on our recommendation that the Administrator of EPA should work collaboratively to identify the indicators that will be used for assessing progress made in improving bay health and clarify how the entities responsible for assessing this progress will coordinate their efforts, EPA noted that it is now working with its federal and state partners to identify measures that will be used to assess bay health, and that this group will make recommendations on which reports will be used to report measures of progress.

The Department of the Interior stated that it does not agree with some of our draft report's findings and recommendations. First, Interior stated that our draft report did not recognize that the Strategy provides a framework to advance the Bay Program beyond the Chesapeake 2000 Agreement. As we noted in our draft report, the Chesapeake Bay Program is a partnership at the federal, state, and local levels. The Strategy provides specific outcomes to be achieved by the federal agencies, but the watershed states have not committed to the Strategy, and most watershed state officials told us that their bay restoration work is conducted according to their commitments to the Chesapeake 2000 Agreement. The report also noted that an alignment action team was formed in June 2010 to work toward aligning Strategy restoration efforts with those of the Bay Program. Second, Interior commented that our report understated the level of collaboration and coordination with the States. We noted in the draft report that federal agencies and watershed states are working on bay issues through the Goal Implementation Teams and that, according to EPA officials, these teams will be used to refine priorities and areas of programmatic focus for the restoration effort. Finally, Interior stated that it believes some of the draft report's findings are based on insufficient information. We have provided detailed responses to this and other Interior comments in appendix VII.

We are sending copies of this report to the appropriate congressional committees, the Administrator of EPA, and other interested parties. In addition, the report will be available at no charge on the GAO website at http://www.gao.gov.

If you or your staff members have any questions about this report, please contact me at (202) 512-3841 or trimbled@gao.gov. Contact points for our Offices of Congressional Relations and Public Affairs may be found on the last page of this report. GAO staff who made major contributions to this report are listed in appendix IX.

David C. Trimble
Director
Natural Resources and Environment

Appendix I: Objectives, Scope, and Methodology

This appendix provides information on the scope of work and the methodology used to determine (1) the extent to which the *Strategy for Protecting and Restoring the Chesapeake Bay Watershed* (the Strategy) includes measurable goals for restoring the Chesapeake Bay that are shared by stakeholders and actions to attain these goals;[1] (2) the key factors, if any, federal and state officials identified that may reduce the likelihood of achieving Strategy goals and actions; and (3) agency plans for assessing progress made in implementing the Strategy and restoring bay health.

To determine the extent to which the Strategy includes measurable goals for restoring the Chesapeake Bay that are shared by stakeholders and actions to attain these goals, we reviewed the Strategy to understand its structure and identify goals and actions. For the actions, we focused on the 116 actions that are designed to lead directly to the Strategy's goals. We did not evaluate an additional 51 actions in the Strategy that were designed to provide cross-cutting support for attaining the goals. We also reviewed previous bay restoration agreements, such as Chesapeake 2000, to identify previous bay restoration goals. In addition, we interviewed officials from each of the federal entities involved in developing and overseeing the implementation of the Strategy, which make up the Federal Leadership Committee: the Departments of Agriculture, Commerce, Defense, Homeland Security, the Interior, and Transportation, and the Environmental Protection Agency (EPA). We also interviewed officials from each of the states in the watershed—Delaware, Maryland, New York, Pennsylvania, Virginia, and West Virginia—and the District of Columbia, collectively referred to as watershed states in this report, and representatives of other Chesapeake Bay organizations, such as the Chesapeake Bay Foundation, to gain an understanding of the Strategy and bay restoration efforts in general.

To determine the key factors federal and state officials identified that may reduce the likelihood of achieving Strategy goals and actions, we first surveyed officials from each of the 11 agencies responsible for creating and implementing the Strategy and received responses from January 2011 through May 2011. These agencies are EPA; the Department of Agriculture's Forest Service and Natural Resources Conservation

---

[1]Federal Leadership Committee for the Chesapeake Bay, *Executive Order 13508 Strategy for Protecting and Restoring the Chesapeake Bay Watershed* (Washington, D.C.: May 2010).

Service; the Department of Commerce's National Oceanic and
Atmospheric Administration; the Department of Defense's Navy and U.S.
Army Corps of Engineers; the Department of Homeland Security; the
Department of the Interior's National Park Service, Fish and Wildlife
Service, and U.S. Geological Survey; and the Department of
Transportation. For each agency, we identified as respondents federal
officials who participated in Strategy development and implementation on
behalf of their agencies, through agency interviews. We used the survey
to obtain and analyze information from each of the agencies about each
action and measurable goal for which the agency had responsibility, and
about each of the Strategy's four broad goals. The questionnaire used for
this study is available in appendix II. We sent the questionnaire by e-mail,
and respondents returned it by e-mail after marking checkboxes or
entering responses into open answer boxes. All of the agencies
responded to our survey.

To identify key factors that could reduce the likelihood of achieving
Strategy goals and actions, we conducted a content analysis of
responses to question 2 from both the actions and measurable goals
portions of the survey. Two analysts independently reviewed the
agencies' responses to each question and together identified the
categories most often cited in these responses. They then coded each
survey response into those categories. In cases where differences
between the two reviewers regarding the coding of responses into content
categories were found, all differences were resolved through reviewer
discussion. Ultimately, there was 100 percent agreement between the
reviewers. See appendix III for further analysis we conducted with survey
data.

Because this was not a sample survey, it has no sampling errors. To
ensure the reliability of the data collected through our survey of the 11
Strategy agencies, we took a number of steps to reduce measurement
error, nonresponse error, and respondent bias. These steps included
conducting three pretests in person prior to distributing the survey to
ensure that our questions were clear, precise, and consistently
interpreted; reviewing responses to identify obvious errors or
inconsistencies; and conducting follow-up interviews with officials to
review and clarify responses. We determined the survey data to be
sufficiently reliable for the purposes of this report.

In addition to conducting the survey mentioned above, we interviewed
officials from each of the watershed states to determine their knowledge
of and involvement with the Strategy; to identify the factors, if any, that

state officials believe could reduce the likelihood of both Strategy and bay restoration success; and to ask about state-related federal official survey responses. We also interviewed a nonprobability sample of individuals who have expertise in the subject matter of the Strategy's measurable goals and solicited their views on the likelihood that the measurable goals could be achieved. We identified these individuals primarily through GAO's prior work on the Chesapeake Bay, and the final list included mostly faculty and staff from the University of Maryland's Center for Environmental Science and the Virginia Institute of Marine Studies. We asked them questions to determine the nature and extent of their expertise, and to ensure that they were not currently or recently employed by EPA and that they had not contributed to the Strategy. We developed a semistructured interview guide containing open-ended questions to solicit responses about their familiarity with the Strategy and the measurable goals that correlated with their area of expertise. We interviewed nearly all of the experts by telephone. Because we used a nonprobability sample, the information obtained from these interviews is not generalizable to other members of academia with bay-related expertise.

To determine the plans in place for assessing the progress of implementing the Strategy and restoring the bay, we reviewed the Strategy and related assessment documents, such as an action plan and a quarterly progress report. We also reviewed several Bay Barometers, annual bay restoration assessment documents issued by the Chesapeake Bay Program.[2] In addition, we interviewed EPA officials who represent the Federal Leadership Committee and the Chesapeake Bay Program Office—the office that represents the federal government with the Chesapeake Bay Program—to discuss how they plan to assess progress on implementing the Strategy and restoring bay health, and also to identify any additional methods EPA plans to use to assess progress in these areas. We also spoke with officials from each of the other Strategy agencies about their roles in assessing Strategy progress.

We conducted this performance audit from August 2010 to September 2011 in accordance with generally accepted government auditing standards. Those standards require that we plan and perform the audit to

---

[2]The Bay Program is a partnership to direct and conduct the restoration of the bay at the federal, state, and local levels that also includes academic institutions and nonprofit organizations.

obtain sufficient, appropriate evidence to provide a reasonable basis for
our findings and conclusions based on our audit objectives. We believe
that the evidence obtained provides a reasonable basis for our findings
and conclusions based on our audit objectives.

Appendix II: Survey Questions

We surveyed officials from each of the federal agencies involved with creating and overseeing the implementation of the Strategy using all of the questions below as stated here. We provided these questions to the officials in a format that identified the Strategy actions, measurable goals, and broad goals for which their agency had responsibility as identified in the Federal Leadership Committee's Fiscal Year 2011 Action Plan.[1]

In our survey, we asked officials from each Strategy agency the following questions regarding each action for which the agency has responsibility:

1. Do you believe this action can be accomplished by the action deadline, assuming current and expected budget and staff levels? (If no deadline is specified, please use the overall Strategy deadline of 2025 as the default deadline.)

- Definitely yes
- Probably yes
- Probably no
- Definitely no
- Don't know
- My agency is not responsible for this action.

1a. Please explain your answer. (For example, please describe whether certain portions of this action are more or less likely to be accomplished by the deadline than others.)

2. What factors do you foresee, if any, that could reduce the likelihood this action will be accomplished? (Please list and briefly describe the factors. This could include factors within or beyond your agency's control.)

3. Is participation from agencies of any of the following state governments necessary for your agency to accomplish this action? (Please check all that apply. Please consider the entire duration of time during which your agency will be working on this action.)

---

[1]Federal Leadership Committee for the Chesapeake Bay, *Fiscal Year 2011 Action Plan* (Washington, D.C.: Sept. 30, 2010).

- Delaware
- District of Columbia
- Maryland
- New York
- Pennsylvania
- Virginia
- West Virginia
- Other (please list in 3a)
- None
- Don't know.

3a. If you checked "Other" in 3, please list the state government(s) necessary for your agency to accomplish this action.

4. If this action were not completed, how would this affect the likelihood of achieving the outcome or goal listed below the drop down box?

- Achieving the outcome or goal would be far less likely
- Achieving the outcome or goal would be somewhat less likely
- Achieving the outcome or goal would be no less likely
- Don't know.

4a. Please explain your answer to 4.

We asked officials from each agency the following questions regarding each measurable goal (which are referred to as outcomes in the Strategy and in our survey questions) that contain an action for which the agency has responsibility. For actions in the water quality broad goal that are listed under more than one measurable goal, we asked the relevant agencies question 4 twice, once for each measurable goal.

1. If all the actions for this outcome (including those for which your agency or other agencies are responsible) are completed, do you believe the outcome will be achieved?

- Definitely yes
- Probably yes
- Probably no
- Definitely no
- Don't know.

1a. Please explain your answer. (For example, please describe whether certain portions of this outcome are more or less likely to be achieved by the deadline than others.)

2. If all the actions for this outcome (including those of your agency and other agencies) are completed, what factors do you foresee, if any, that could reduce the likelihood that this outcome will be achieved? (Please list and briefly describe the factors. This could include factors within or beyond your agency's control.)

3. How important is this outcome to attaining the goal listed below the drop down box?

- Very important
- Somewhat important
- Not at all important
- Don't know.

We asked officials from each agency the following questions regarding each broad goal (which are referred to as goals in the Strategy and in the survey) that contain an action for which the agency has responsibility.

1. If all of the outcomes for this goal are achieved, do you believe the goal will be attained?

- Definitely yes
- Probably yes
- Probably no
- Definitely no
- Don't know.

1a. Please explain your answer.

2. How important is achieving this goal to restoring the overall health of the bay?

- Very important
- Somewhat important
- Not at all important
- Don't know.

We asked officials from each agency the following general questions.

1. Please provide any additional comments you may have about the Strategy or your responses in this data collection instrument.

2. Please list any actions for which your agency is responsible that we did not ask about.

Appendix III: Collaboration Needed between Federal Agencies and Watershed States to Accomplish Strategy Actions

Collaboration between federal agencies and the watershed states will be required to complete many of the Strategy actions. In response to question 3 of the actions portion of our survey, federal officials identified Strategy actions that require state participation in order to accomplish the actions. In those cases where federal officials reported that state participation was necessary to accomplish the action, the officials identified the necessary state or states. Figure 3 shows the extent of collaboration that will be needed between federal agencies and watershed states to accomplish Strategy actions. Each node represents a federal agency or a state. Each link between a pair of nodes indicates that the corresponding entities will need to collaborate to accomplish an action. Thicker links indicate more extensive collaboration because of the number of times federal officials identified participation from a particular state as necessary. Table 3 shows the number of actions for which each federal agency reported that participation from a watershed state was necessary to accomplish the action.

Figure 3: Extent of Collaboration Needed between Federal Agencies and Watershed States to Accomplish Strategy Actions

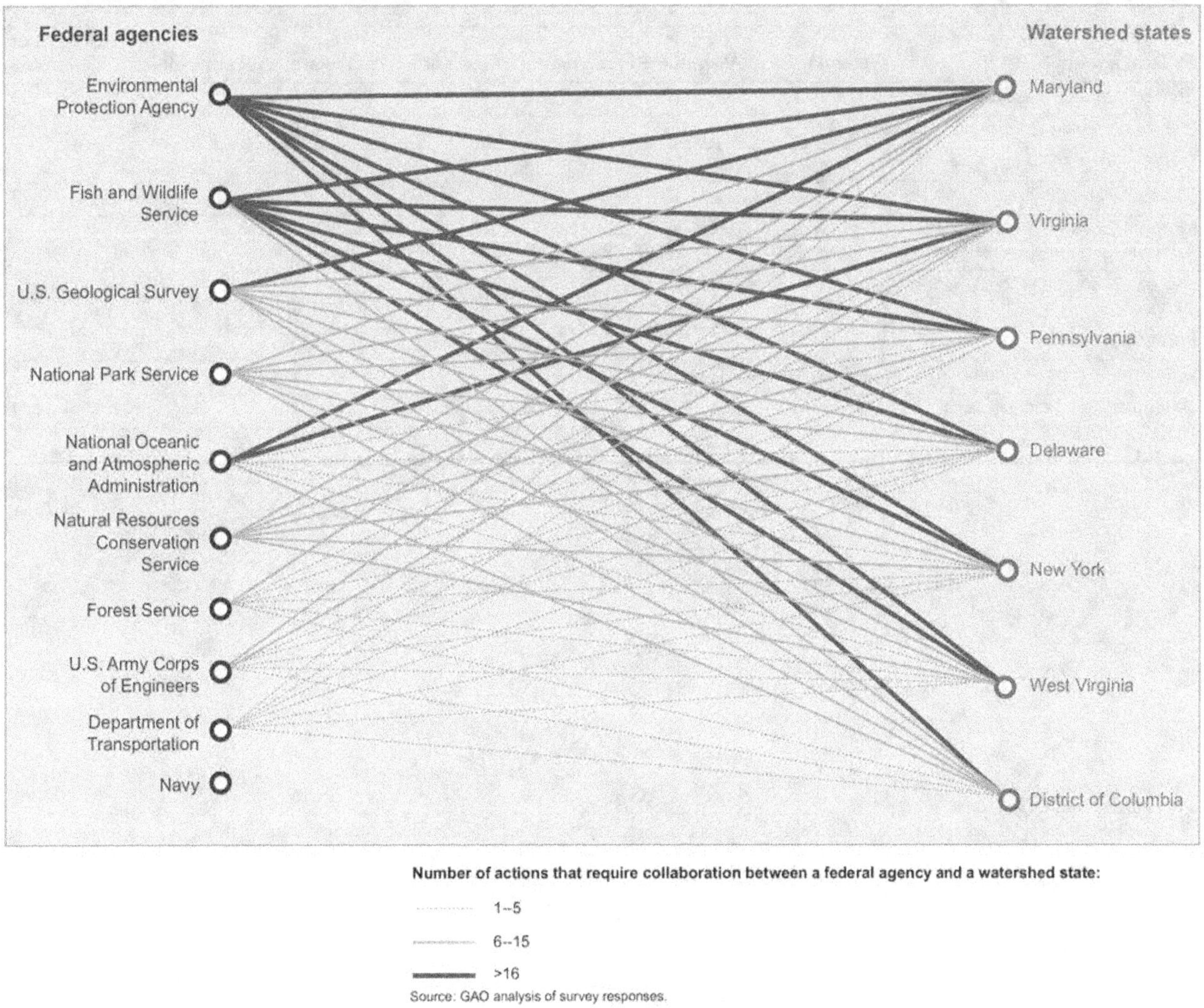

Number of actions that require collaboration between a federal agency and a watershed state:

.... 1--5

─ ─ ─ ─ ─ 6--15

━━━━━ >16

Source: GAO analysis of survey responses.

Table 3: Number of Actions for Which Each Federal Agency Reported That Participation from a Watershed State Was Necessary to Accomplish the Action

Federal agency	Maryland	Virginia	Pennsylvania	New York	Delaware	West Virginia	District of Columbia
Environmental Protection Agency	20	19	19	19	19	19	20
Fish and Wildlife Service	24	24	19	18	19	18	6
U.S. Geological Survey	19	14	14	9	11	10	9
National Park Service	12	12	11	10	11	10	12
National Oceanic and Atmospheric Administration	22	22	3	3	3	1	8
Natural Resources Conservation Service	9	9	9	8	8	8	0
Forest Service	6	5	5	5	5	5	1
U.S. Army Corps of Engineers	12	8	4	2	1	1	1
Department of Transportation	4	4	4	4	4	4	4
Navy	0	0	0	0	0	0	0

Source: GAO analysis of survey responses.

Appendix IV: Chesapeake Bay Program Adaptive Management Decision Framework

The Chesapeake Bay program approved the following adaptive management decision framework on May 10, 2011, as an incremental step in moving toward adaptive management:

1. Articulate program goals.
   Identify the goals the goal implementation team is working toward.

2. Describe factors influencing goal attainment.
   Identify and prioritize all factors that influence performance toward a goal. This step can help identify areas for cross-goal implementation team collaboration.

3. Assess current management efforts (and gaps).
   Identification of gaps/overlaps in existing management programs addressing the important factors affecting goal attainment.

4. Develop management strategy.
   Coordination and implementation planning by stakeholders.

5. Develop monitoring program.

6. Assess performance.
   Criteria for success/failure of management efforts should be known when the strategy is developed and the monitoring program is designed. This is the analysis that informs program adaptation. This helps inform next steps.

7. Manage adaptively.
   Based on the monitoring assessment, system models are amended, and monitoring strategies are revised to improve program performance.

UNITED STATES ENVIRONMENTAL PROTECTION AGENCY
WASHINGTON D.C. 20460

SEP - 7 2011

Mr. David C. Trimble
Director
Natural Resources and Environment
U.S. Government Accountability Office
Washington, D.C. 20548

Dear Mr. Trimble:

Thank you for the opportunity to review and comment on the draft report *Chesapeake Bay: Restoration Effort Needs Common Federal and State Goals and Assessment Approach*, which examines recent developments in the Chesapeake Bay Program and offers four recommendations. The U.S. Environmental Protection Agency is in general agreement with all four recommendations, and we are pleased to share some thoughts in this letter and more detailed comments in an attached document.

First recommendation: The Chesapeake Bay Program should develop common bay restoration goals to help ensure that federal and state restoration stakeholders are working toward the same goals.

The EPA's Response: As the report notes, with the completion dates for most of the commitments in the Chesapeake 2000 Agreement set for 2010 or before and with the direction from President Barack Obama to develop a strategy for implementing Executive Order 13508 *Chesapeake Bay Protection and Restoration*, there is a new complexity regarding programmatic goals. The draft report highlights instances of this complexity, but does not highlight instances where common goals and common directions are already present in the Chesapeake Bay Program.

For instance, improving water quality, a goal that includes measurable parameters, is supported by the Bay watershed jurisdictions and is being implemented through the Chesapeake Bay total maximum daily load and the jurisdictions' watershed implementation plans. The states might have been unable to commit to the specific metric and time frame associated with many of the outcomes at this point. However, they did agree to work with the federal agencies through a process agreed to by the Chesapeake Executive Council and the Federal Leadership Committee for the Chesapeake Bay that will immediately begin to set goals and areas of programmatic and geographic focus through the Chesapeake Bay Program's goal implementation teams and will be guided by key strategies and agreements, such as *Chesapeake 2000*, Executive Council directives and the Executive Order strategy.

If the leadership deems a new agreement is necessary to ensure commitment to these goals and priorities, they have further committed to develop a new agreement no later than the 2013 Executive Council meeting. For details on the full agreement on aligning the Executive Order goals with the Chesapeake Bay Program Partnership, please see the attached *Coordinating Chesapeake Bay Program and Federal Leadership Committee Goals, Outcomes and Actions*.

Second recommendation: The Chesapeake Bay Program should establish milestones for gauging progress toward measurable goals for the entire restoration effort.

The EPA's Response: As discussed in the draft report, the bay watershed jurisdictions have developed two-year milestones, and the federal agency partners are developing two-year milestones that will cover 2012 and 2013. The EPA believes that the goals established in the Executive Order strategy provide important targets to be achieved by meeting the two-year milestones. Agencies and other stakeholders will be able to measure progress toward those targets to determine whether adequate progress is being made.

Finally, the EPA believes that while a blueprint of milestones through 2025 would be useful, such a document would do little to ensure that each milestone would be met, particularly given the current climate of budgetary uncertainty. While we agree that a general blueprint that highlights the approach used for meeting restoration goals through 2025 is important – assuming that there will be a slower start that will accelerate later, that there will be steady rate of implementation over time or that there will be faster implementation at first and slowing later – we do not wish to limit our ability for adaptive management by locking in a too-detailed plan for the entire time period.

Third recommendation: The Chesapeake Bay Program should develop an adaptive management program that will allow restoration stakeholders to evaluate progress made in restoring the bay and adjust actions as needed.

The EPA's Response: The EPA acknowledges that this concern has been raised in previous GAO reports and in the recent National Academy of Science's report on the program. The EPA and its program partners are continuing to more clearly articulate and institutionalize an adaptive management process throughout the program. In May 2011, the Chesapeake Bay Program's principals' staff committee adopted a decision-support framework that enables effective adaptive management in the Chesapeake Bay Program. It was later endorsed by the Chesapeake Bay Program's leadership at the July 2011 Executive Council Meeting. The framework is a seven-step process that articulates program goals, describes factors influencing goal attainment, assesses current management efforts and gaps, develops a management strategy, develops a monitoring program, assesses performance and manages adaptively.

An important step in the implementation of this approach is the development of Chesapeake*Stat*, a Web-based decision-support tool that provides a wealth of environmental, financial and other information for all aspects of the Chesapeake Bay Program. To pilot this approach prior to the July 2011 Executive Council meeting, two goal implementation teams used Chesapeake*Stat* to collect, analyze and enter information on particular goals – reducing pollution related to agricultural practices and restoring underwater grasses – into the decision framework so they can begin to use adaptive management to support decision making. The Executive Council agreed that the Chesapeake Bay Program would use this framework when aligning the Executive Order strategy goals with the program. This is an area in which the program will continue to improve.

Fourth recommendation: The Chesapeake Bay Program should identify the indicators that will be used for assessing progress made in improving bay health and clarify how the entities responsible for assessing this progress will coordinate their efforts.

The EPA's Response: The Chesapeake Bay Program is always exploring better and more complete ways to use information and indicators to report on the health of the Chesapeake Bay, its rivers and the watershed. New indicators for outcomes not currently described in *Chesapeake 2000* will be used as part of the adaptive management process described above. Through the Chesapeake Bay Program, the EPA and its federal and state partners are now working on identifying measures that will be used to assess the health of the bay, the rivers and the watershed and identifying measures of progress being made by federal and state partners to improve bay health. The group will also make recommendations on which reports, such as Bay Barometer and the Executive Order Progress Report, will be used to report measures of progress. The EPA is advocating for inclusion of all of these measures in Chesapeake*Stat* so that any interested party will be able to review our progress in a transparent and timely manner.

Finally, we appreciate the thoughtful work of the Government Accountability Office's staff members during this review and their constructive engagement with Chesapeake Bay Program Office staff members and representatives of our partner agencies and jurisdictions.

Sincerely,

Bob Perciasepe

Attachments

Appendix VI: Comments from the Department of Homeland Security

U.S. Department of Homeland Security
Washington, DC 20528

Homeland
Security

September 1, 2011

David C. Trimble
Director, Natural Resources and Environment
441 G Street, NW
U.S. Government Accountability Office
Washington, DC 20548

Re: Draft Report GAO-11-802, "CHESAPEAKE BAY: Restoration Effort Needs Common
        Federal and State Goals and Assessment Approach"

Dear Mr. Trimble:

Thank you for the opportunity to review and comment on this draft report. The U.S. Department
of Homeland Security (DHS) appreciates the U.S. Government Accountability Office's (GAO's)
work in planning and conducting its review and issuing this report.

The Department is pleased to note GAO's positive acknowledgment of many Federal Leadership
Committee efforts related to restoring and protecting the Chesapeake Bay. Although the report
does not contain any recommendations directed at DHS, the Department remains committed to
continuing its collaboration with partners, such as the Environmental Protection Agency, and the
U.S. Departments of Agriculture, Commerce, and Interior, among others to improve the health of
the bay.

Again, thank you for the opportunity to review and comment on this draft report. We look
forward to working with you on future homeland security issues.

Sincerely,

Jim H. Crumpacker
Director
Departmental GAO-OIG Liaison Office

Appendix VII: Comments from the Department of the Interior

Note: GAO comments supplementing those in the report text appear at the end of this appendix.

 United States Department of the Interior
OFFICE OF THE SECRETARY
Washington, DC 20240

TAKE PRIDE
IN AMERICA

AUG 3 1 2011

Mr. David Trimble
Director, Natural Resources and Environment
U.S. Government Accountability Office
441 G Street, N.W.
Washington, D.C. 20548

Dear Mr. Trimble:

The Department of the Interior (DOI) has reviewed the draft Government Accountability Office (GAO) report titled *CHESAPEAKE BAY: Restoration Effort Needs Common Federal and State Goals and Assessment Approach (GAO-11-802)*. The DOI does not agree with some of the findings and recommendations in the draft report. Our primary concerns include:

- The GAO draft report does not recognize that the May 2010 *Strategy for Protecting and Restoring the Chesapeake Bay* provides a framework to advance the Chesapeake Bay Program beyond the outdated and expired commitments in the Chesapeake 2000 agreement.

- GAO understates the level of collaboration and coordination with the States.

- We believe that some of the draft report's findings are based on insufficient information.

Enclosed are detailed comments on the findings and recommendations.

We hope these comments will assist you in preparing the final report. If you have any questions, or need additional information, please contact David Russ at (703) 648-6660, Scott Phillips at (443) 498-5552, John Maounis at (410) 260-2471 or Mike Slattery at (410) 260-2487.

Sincerely,

Pamela Hare (Acting For)

Rhea Suh
Assistant Secretary
Policy, Management and Budget

Enclosure

Enclosure

**Department of the Interior Comments in Response to the GAO Draft Report
CHESAPEAKE BAY: Restoration Effort Needs Common Federal and State Goals and
Assessment Approach**

Specific comments on GAO findings

GAO Finding: Restoration *Strategy* Includes Measureable Goals and Action to Achieve Them,
but Not All Bay Restoration Stakeholders are Working Toward These Goals (p. 10-15).

See comment 1.

Comments: The May 2010 *Strategy for Protecting and Restoring the Chesapeake Bay
Watershed (Strategy)* offers the next generation of specific outcomes to be achieved by the
Chesapeake Bay Program (CBP). Most of the specific outcomes in the Chesapeake 2000
agreement have expired. The *Strategy* outcomes were developed, as directed in the President's
Chesapeake Bay Executive Order, to move the program forward. Federal partners, in
consultation with States, worked to develop new outcomes to guide the program for the future
(2025), building upon the general goals of the existing Chesapeake 2000 agreement. The
Strategy adds measurable watershed outcomes, which were developed with the States.
Modifications were made, based on State comments. However, the States chose not to formally
adopt the new outcomes. One reason for States' not adopting the new outcomes was that their
primary focus was on meeting their regulatory requirements under the Total Maximum Daily
Load (TMDL) process. The States' Watershed Implementation Plans for the TMDL were also
due in 2010. We agree that common, measureable goals are ideal, but we are not in a position to
force State participation. The CBP Principal Staff Committee (PSC) directed the five Goal
Teams to align the commitments in the Chesapeake 2000 agreement with the *Strategy* outcomes.
This will result in a shared set of goals for all partners by 2013.

GAO Finding: Federal and State Officials Identified Three Key Factors that May Reduce the
Likelihood of Achieving *Strategy* Goals and Actions (p. 16-19).

Comments: Federal agencies have made progress on the three areas identified by GAO—
collaboration, funding constraints, and external phenomena.

See comment 2.

Federal and State partners consulted through the Bay Program Committee structure on the
Strategy and associated goals. This structure includes the PSC, the Management Board, the Goal
Implementation Teams, and the Advisory Committees. The *Strategy* was discussed at three PSC
meetings during 2009 and 2010, and at another two-day meeting in February 2010. The PSC
consists of representatives from eight Federal agencies and 19 State agencies from
all major jurisdictions in the watershed (six States and the District of Columbia), and the
Chesapeake Bay Commission. The *Strategy* was also discussed at the meetings of the five Goal
Implementation Teams and the three Advisory Committees (Citizens, Local Governments, and
Science) between 2009 and 2010.

1

Since the Strategy was released in May 2010, Federal and State collaboration has continued through the PSC, with more direct collaboration on *Strategy* outcomes within the five CBP Goal Teams and the Science Support Team. State and Federal partners share leadership of the five Goal Teams, which meet at least every other month. Each Goal Team is focusing on specific Federal and State actions to meet the Chesapeake 2000 goals and to address the new *Strategy* outcomes.

Funding constraints are a legitimate concern. The President's requested budgets in both 2011 and 2012 would have adequately supported the actions in the *Strategy*. However, Congress did not appropriate funds at the requested level in 2011. Appropriations for 2012 are pending Congressional action. Based on initial House action, there is a high probability of reduced budgets. As a result, some actions cannot move forward. The Federal agencies have prioritized actions to maximize progress toward achieving the *Strategy* goals. Constraints on State budgets will also slow progress on CBP goals.

As a result, some actions cannot move forward. The Federal agencies have prioritized actions to maximize progress toward achieving the *Strategy* goals. Constraints on State budgets will also slow progress on CBP goals.

See comment 3.

We agree with the GAO finding that external phenomena, including climate change, could have an effect on achieving the *Strategy*'s goals. However, the GAO did not review or take into account the *Strategy* chapter describing how the Federal agencies propose to adapt to climate change. These proposals include conducting vulnerability assessments and monitoring. The resulting information will help State and Federal partners adapt to climate change. The CBP is addressing climate change through the Scientific and Technical Advisory Committee (STAC), which is comprised of Federal agencies and academic institutions. The STAC meets quarterly. In addition, a STAC workshop held in March 2011 brought together Federal, State, and academic partners to develop actions to address climate change.

GAO Finding: Agency Plans for Assessing Progress on Implementing the Strategy and Restoring Bay Health are Limited or Not Fully Developed, and it is Unclear What Indicators Will be Used to Assess Progress on Bay Health (p. 20-24).

Specific GAO Finding: Milestone Development Plan is Limited.

See comment 4.

Comments: We disagree with the GAO's recommendation for a blueprint of milestones for the entire restoration effort (2011-2025). The 12 outcomes provide the blueprint for the long-term success of the program. The two-year milestones provide an adaptive management approach to implement plans, assess progress, and make adjustments as more is learned (see next comment).

Specific GAO Finding: Plans for Adaptive Management and Annual Progress Report are Not Fully Developed.

See comment 5.

Comments: The GAO did not include information on the CBP's *Decision Framework*, which was adopted by State and Federal partners in May 2011. The *Decision Framework* is a six-step adaptive management process focused on defining goals, implementing actions, monitoring

2

See comment 6.

See comment 7.

progress, and making adjustments. The new adaptive management process was based on several documents, including information in the "Strengthening Science" chapter of the *Strategy*.

The 2011 *Strategy* progress report is on schedule to be completed by January 2012. An outline for the progress report was approved by CEQ and OMB on August 12, 2011. The performance data for the progress report is the quarterly information reported by the Federal agencies. GAO's concern about the performance information (page 22 of the GAO draft) relates primarily to the Federal agencies' uncertainty under the continuing resolution. The performance information was refined when Congress passed a final 2011 appropriation.

<u>Specific GAO Finding</u>: It is unclear what indicators will be used to assess Bay health.

<u>Comments</u>: Federal and State partners will continue to work to improve the CBP publication, *Bay Barometer*, which reports on the overall health of the Bay. New indicators for outcomes not previously used in Chesapeake 2000 will be added, as necessary, as part of the adaptive management process. The CBP has a team in place (not two groups as suggested by the GAO draft report) to improve the *Bay Barometer* for the next reporting cycle. The team will recommend to the CBP partners (both Federal and State) any changes to the indicators to assess Bay health.

3

GAO Comments

1. Interior commented that the Strategy offers the next generation of specific outcomes to be achieved by the Chesapeake Bay Program, which is a partnership at the federal, state, and local levels. As we noted in our draft report, the Strategy provides specific outcomes to be achieved by the federal agencies. In addition, we noted that the watershed states are critical partners in the restoration effort, and federal officials reported that watershed state action will be necessary to accomplish 96 of the 116 Strategy actions. However, the watershed states have not committed to the Strategy, and officials from most of the states told us that they are generally unaware of what federal agencies may require from them to implement the Strategy. In addition, we noted in the draft report that most watershed state officials told us that their bay restoration work is conducted according to their commitments to the Chesapeake 2000 Agreement. The Strategy recognizes the need to integrate the goals of the Chesapeake Bay Program with those of the Strategy. We noted in our draft report that the Federal Leadership Committee and the Bay Program created an alignment action team in June 2010 to work toward aligning Strategy restoration efforts with those of the Bay Program, including Chesapeake 2000 Agreement efforts.

2. Interior commented that we understated the level of collaboration and coordination with the states, and it provided information on the Bay Program structure and meetings through which collaboration takes place. As we reported, most of the federal officials we surveyed indicated that a potential lack of collaboration among stakeholders could reduce the likelihood of achieving Strategy goals and actions. We did not comment in our draft report on the extent to which the federal agencies and watershed states collaborated in the development of the Strategy. We noted in the draft report that the federal agencies and watershed states are working on bay issues through the Goal Implementation Teams and that, according to EPA officials, bay restoration stakeholders plan to use these teams to refine priorities and areas of programmatic focus, guided by the Chesapeake 2000 Agreement and the Strategy.

3. Interior commented that we did not review or take into account the Strategy chapter describing how the federal agencies propose to adapt to climate change. In our draft report, we noted that the Strategy identifies four supporting strategies, including respond to climate change, and 51 actions associated with these strategies. In addition, we reported that federal officials told us that effects of

external phenomena, such as climate change, beyond what was
planned for in developing the Strategy could affect the likelihood of
achieving the measurable goals.

4. Interior disagreed with our recommendation to EPA to work with
   federal and state bay restoration stakeholders to establish milestones
   for gauging progress toward measurable goals for the entire
   restoration effort. Interior further commented that the 12 measurable
   goals provide a blueprint for the long-term success of the program. As
   we noted in the draft report, the 12 measurable goals contain numeric
   descriptions of results to be achieved by 2025. However, these
   measurable goals do not provide a blueprint of milestones to be met
   prior to 2025 that would allow the agencies to determine whether they
   are on track to meet these measurable goals. We agree that 2-year
   milestones can contribute to an adaptive management approach, and
   as we noted in the draft report, a blueprint of milestones for the entire
   restoration effort can allow the agencies to show when the actions are
   expected to result in progress toward the measurable goals,
   determine whether the actions are having their intended results, and
   make changes to these actions as needed.

5. Interior commented that we did not include information on the Bay
   Program's seven-step adaptive management decision framework. In
   response to this comment, we modified the report to include
   information about this framework. However, as we note in the report,
   this framework was developed for the Bay Program and does not
   include clear linkages to the Strategy actions and measurable goals. It
   is unclear how it will be used by the Federal Leadership Committee
   agencies to adaptively manage Strategy actions and meet Strategy
   goals. In August 2011, EPA officials told us that a fully developed
   adaptive management process is needed.

6. Interior commented that the annual progress report is on schedule to
   be completed by January 2012 and that the Council on Environmental
   Quality and Office of Management and Budget approved an outline for
   the report on August 12, 2011. According to an EPA official, the
   outline that Interior refers to in its comments did not address what
   performance information will be collected. We continue to believe that
   plans for the annual progress report are not fully developed.

7. Interior commented that a Bay Program team is working to improve
   the Bay Barometer publication, which reports on the overall health of
   the bay. We noted in our draft report that there are two groups that

plan to assess bay health. The Federal Leadership Committee will review indicators of environmental conditions in the bay through its annual progress report, and the Bay Program will report on bay health and restoration efforts through its Bay Barometer. As we reported, the content of the next Bay Barometer report has not yet been determined, and it is unclear if the groups will assess the same or different indicators of progress.

Appendix VIII: Comments from the State of New York

New York State Department of Environmental Conservation
Assistant Commissioner
Office of Water Resources, 14th Floor
625 Broadway, Albany, New York 12233-1010
Phone: (518) 402-2794 • Fax: (518) 402-8541
Website: www.dec.ny.gov

Joe Martens
Commissioner

August 25, 2011

Mr. David Trimble
Director, Natural Resources and Environment
United States Government Accountability Office
441 G Street, NW
Washington, DC 20548

Dear Director Trimble:

On behalf of the State of New York I am submitting the enclosed comments on the draft report: "*Chesapeake Bay Restoration Effort Needs Common Federal and State Goals and Assessment Approach*". New York appreciates the opportunity to provide comments and would like to take this occasion to recognize the efforts of the Environmental Protection Agency (EPA) to understand the characteristics unique to the New York portion of the Chesapeake Bay watershed. Without a doubt, the implementation of Executive Order 13508 and the Chesapeake Bay Total Maximum Daily Load (TMDL) continues to be a challenging effort for EPA and the affected states, including New York. A common-sense approach that ensures that the most cost effective reductions are being put into place will protect the local economy and keep farmers farming.

It is important to recognize the enormity of the Chesapeake Bay restoration effort. Funds for locally-led implementation efforts are being stretched during tough economic times. EPA has recognized the situation of the States and has come forward with capacity grants for regulatory agencies and implementation grants for local conservation efforts. Importantly, in granting these federal funds EPA has been sensitive to the needs of both the immediate Chesapeake Bay States and the Headwater States. New York strongly urges Administrator Jackson to continue her advocacy of funds to address the failing wastewater infrastructure needs across the country as she did in her testimony before Congress on the FY 2011 budget. The need for substantially higher appropriations for the Water Resources Development Act, Clean Water State Revolving Fund, and United States Department of Agriculture Rural Development financial support programs has increased in New York State's portion of the Chesapeake Bay watershed as a result of the Chesapeake Bay TMDL.

New York recognizes the importance of restoring water quality in the Chesapeake Bay and appreciates the challenges faced by federal agencies in implementing Executive Order 13508 and the Chesapeake Bay TMDL. You can be assured that New York will continue its effective efforts to protect water resources within its borders, as well as water quality downstream in the Chesapeake Bay. It is clear that a continued, and heightened, commitment of federal fiscal

2.

resources will be central to the success of this Presidential initiative. Department staff, along with key partners at the New York State Department of Agriculture and Markets and Upper Susquehanna Coalition, look forward to continuing to work with federal, state and local partners to marshal the implementation of on-the-ground projects that will succeed in reducing nutrient and sediment pollution in New York's Susquehanna and Chemung River Basins.

Thank you for the opportunity to provide comments on the draft report: "*Chesapeake Bay Restoration Effort Needs Common Federal and State Goals and Assessment Approach.*" Please direct any questions you may have concerning these comments to Jacqueline Lendrum at (518) 402-8118 or jmlendru@gw.dec.state.ny.us.

Sincerely,

James M. Tierney

Appendix IX: GAO Contact and Staff Acknowledgments

Contact	David C. Trimble, (202) 512-3841 or trimbled@gao.gov
Staff Acknowledgments	In addition to the individual named above, Barbara Patterson, Assistant Director; Lucas Alvarez; Elizabeth Beardsley; Mark Braza; Russ Burnett; David Dornisch; Lina Khan; Marietta Mayfield Revesz; Ben Shouse; Kiki Theodoropoulos; and Michelle K. Treistman made significant contributions to this report. Elizabeth H. Curda and Kim S. Frankena also made important contributions to this report.